Lică Sain

P. OINQUE ENCYCLOPÆDIA

SCULEANCA – SEATTLE
2015

THIS EDITION
PUBLISHED BY
ARRANGEMENT
WITH PROF.
W.W.WOOF

Images & text: Lică Sainciuc

Contributions:

Vasile Sainciuc
George Rusu Ciobanu
Doroteea Elisabeta
Didi
Gabriela Condrea

Layout, images and text © 2015 Lică Sainciuc
First Moldovan edition 1988
Published by *Paint with Words Press*

Printed in the United States of America

All questions and requests should be sent to *p.oinque.me@gmail.com*

ISBN 978-0-9839063-2-2

EXPLANATORY NOTES

Mr. P. Oinque (short for Pig Oink) is an artist, poet and philosopher. Due to his involvement in artistic and philosophical speculations he has little time for washing. Therefore, his closest friends are Buzzy, Wizzy and Zoommy, who provide him support for solving trans-rational quests, namely mind untwisting.

Answers to rational problems (those generating headaches) are provided by Prof. W.W.Woof, who knows everything there is to know. Prof. W.W.Woof has a very noble lineage: in his veins runs the blood of dogs of very many different breeds.

There are questions of everyday life as well. In this case one should address Mylkee.

Mörl Klimber, a qualified roof ascendant.

Esq. Weak is a very distant relative of Mörl Klimber, a relationship not even seriously considered by the latter. But Esq. Weak is in possession of numerous fairy tales heard from ancestors at the fireplace, which make Mörl Klimber squint and purr.

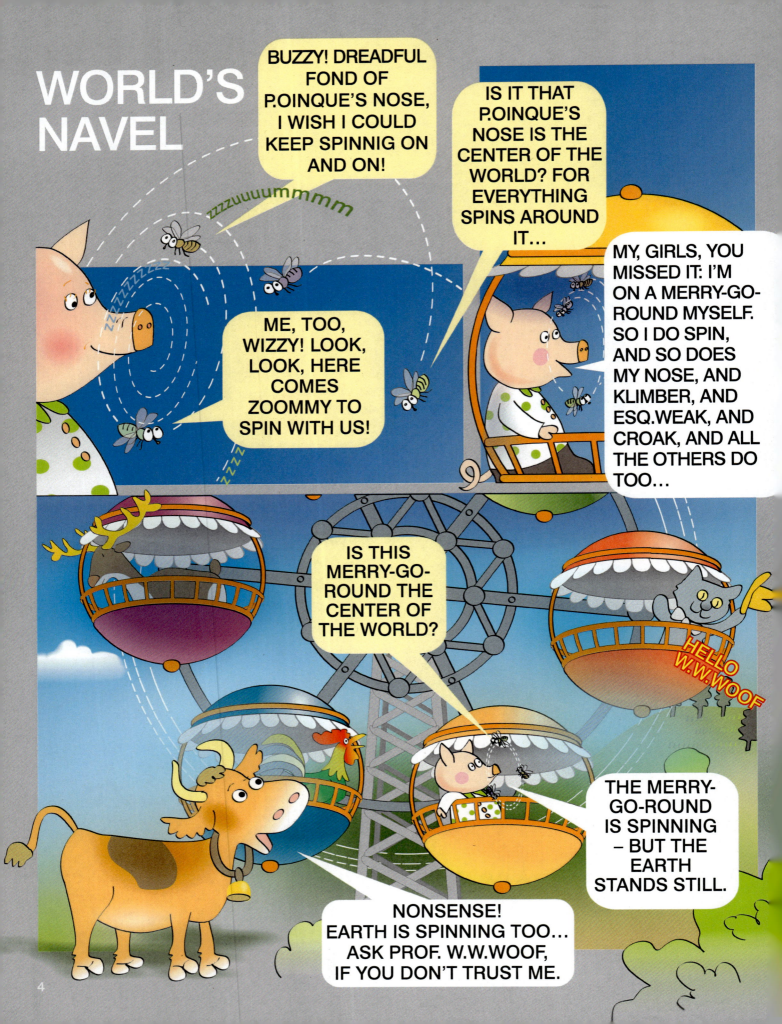

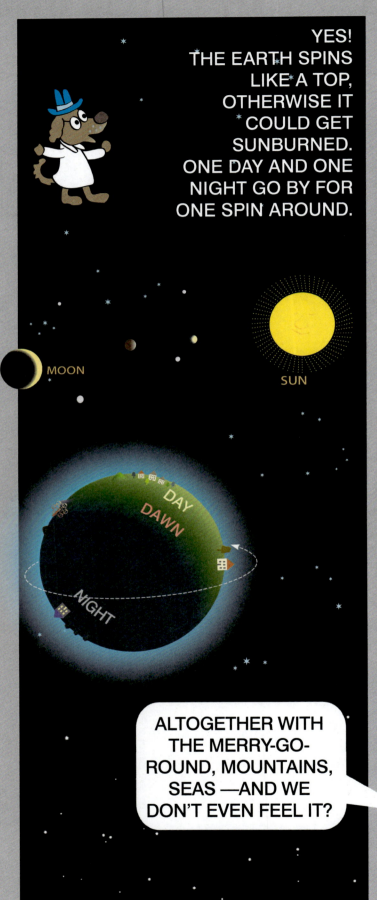

NIGHT

SUNRISE

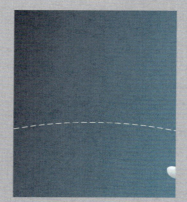
ORBIT

DAY

RAINING

NEWS

CLOUDING

AVIATION

CITY

FOREST

ENTERTAINMENT

COUNTRY

GRAZING

EXPLANATION

POPULATION

WAY

POPULATION

SPROUT

P. OINQUE ONCE HAPPENED TO LIVE ON THE 8TH FLOOR OF AN APARTMENT BUILDING.
HE HAD TROUBLE ADMIRING PLANTS FROM SO HIGH UP.

I WISH I HAD A PLANT OF MY OWN HERE

ONE POT AND ONE BUTTERCUP SEED, PLEASE!

THE POT I CAN GIVE YOU RIGHT NOW. AS TO THE SEED… THE SHELF'S BEEN KNOCKED DOWN, THEY'RE ALL MIXED UP. WOULD YOU COME IN TOMORROW?

P. OINQUE COULD NOT WAIT ANY LONGER.
HE PICKED THE SMALLEST SEEDLET OUT OF THE HEAP, TOOK THE POT AND WENT HOME.

HE FILLED THE POT WITH SOIL, MADE A HOLE WITH HIS STOUT, AND PLANTED THE SEED IN.

HE KEPT WATERING AND WAITING

IN A FEW DAYS …

WELCOME BUTTERCUP!

A WEEK PASSED

PERHAPS IT'S A DANDELION

AFTER A MONTH

A GERANIUM?

IS IT A HOLLYHOCK …?

MAYBE IT'S A SUN-FLOWER

IN A FEW MONTHS… THE PLANT DIDN'T FIT IN THE POT. P. OINQUE HAD TO MOVE IT INTO A BOX.

A MUSTARD BUSH?

A YEAR PASSED…

THE PLANT DIDN'T FIT IN THE ROOM EITHER…

LET US GIVE YOU A HAND! YOU WON'T DO IT ALONE.

IT'S HEAVY!

OH BOTHER! PERHAPS IT IS A TREE.

I HAVE TO PLANT IT OUTDOORS.

EASY! EASY! YOU MEN TAKE IT FROM THERE, AND I'LL PUSH IT FROM HERE...

A BEECH-TREE, FIR-TREE AND PINE-TREE MAY REACH THE AGE OF 400 YEARS

THE OAK AND LIME LIVE UP TO 1000 YEARS

AN AGE OF A WALNUT MAY REACH 2000 YEARS

PROBLEM:

IF: it takes 60 years for an oak-sprout to grow up and 16 years for a human-sprout to grow up,

THEN: how much thought does it take a grown-up human to chop down in a quarter of an hour an oak tree as tall as a building?

OAK

MAPLE

ACACIA

SUNROSE

WILLOW

HAZEL

BIRCH

BEECH

FIR

PINE

LIME

CHESTNUT

MULBERRY

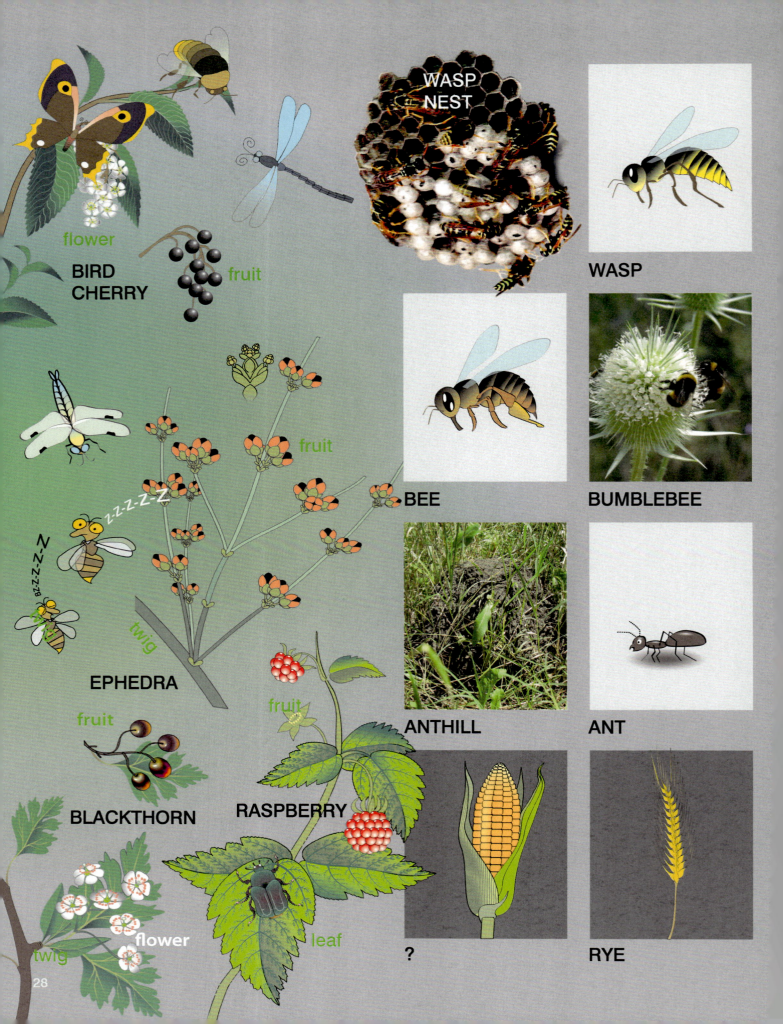

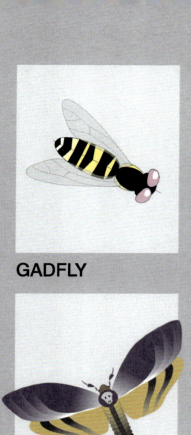   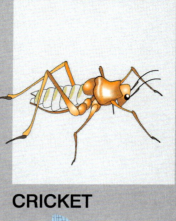

GADFLY   REDBUG   CRICKET

BUTTERFLY   FLY   DRAGONFLY

LADYBUG   WATER STICK   PRAYING BUG   ROACH

LOCUST   GRASSHOPPER   STINKBUG

LONG-HORNED beetle **RHINOCEROS beetle** **beech LONG-HORNED** **TAILOR WASP**

COLORADO bug **COCKCHAFER** **SCARAB** **DOR beetle**

WEEVIL **LOUSE**

Melasoma populi

CROSS SPIDER

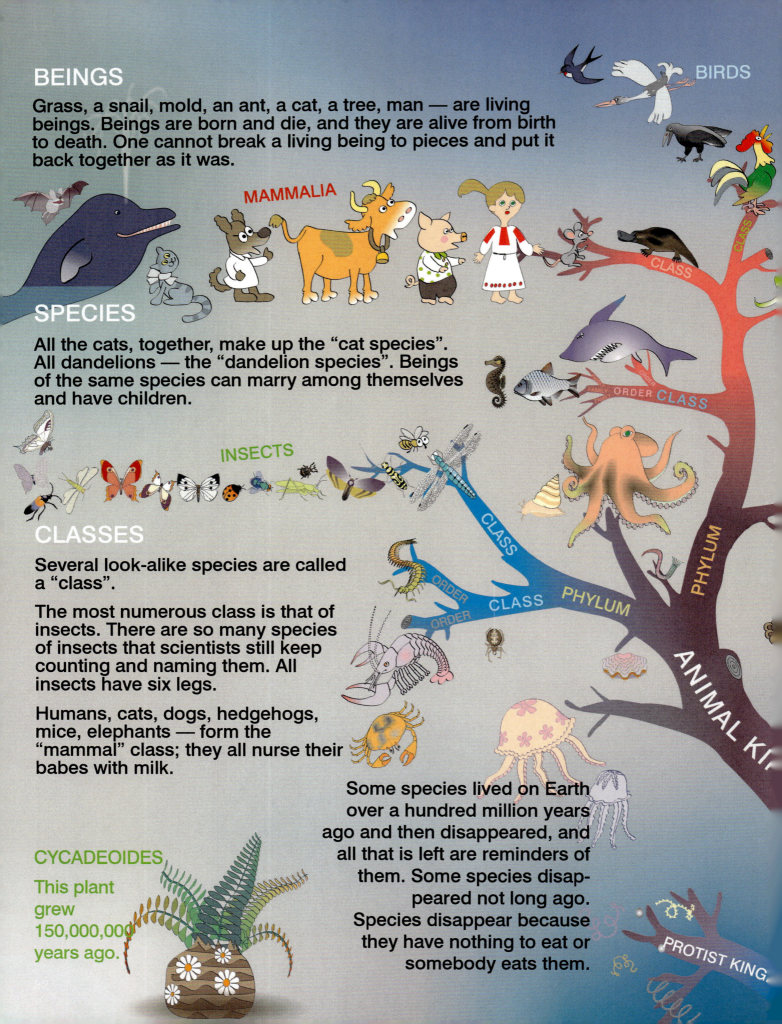

BEINGS

Grass, a snail, mold, an ant, a cat, a tree, man — are living beings. Beings are born and die, and they are alive from birth to death. One cannot break a living being to pieces and put it back together as it was.

SPECIES

All the cats, together, make up the "cat species". All dandelions — the "dandelion species". Beings of the same species can marry among themselves and have children.

CLASSES

Several look-alike species are called a "class".

The most numerous class is that of insects. There are so many species of insects that scientists still keep counting and naming them. All insects have six legs.

Humans, cats, dogs, hedgehogs, mice, elephants — form the "mammal" class; they all nurse their babes with milk.

Some species lived on Earth over a hundred million years ago and then disappeared, and all that is left are reminders of them. Some species disappeared not long ago. Species disappear because they have nothing to eat or somebody eats them.

CYCADEOIDES

This plant grew 150,000,000 years ago.

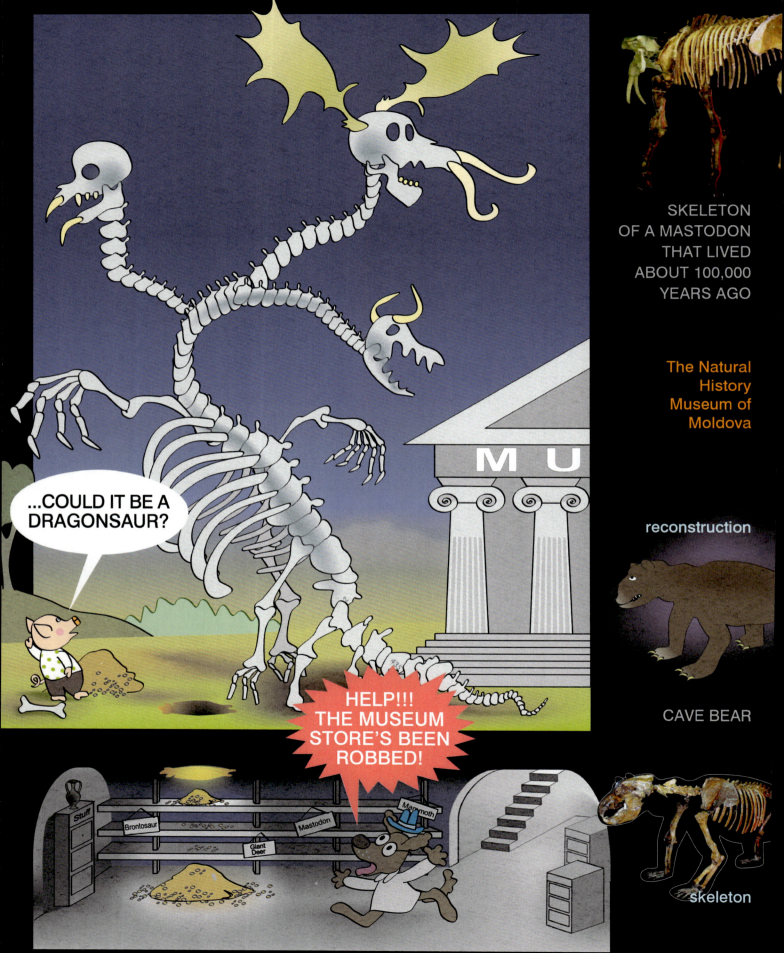

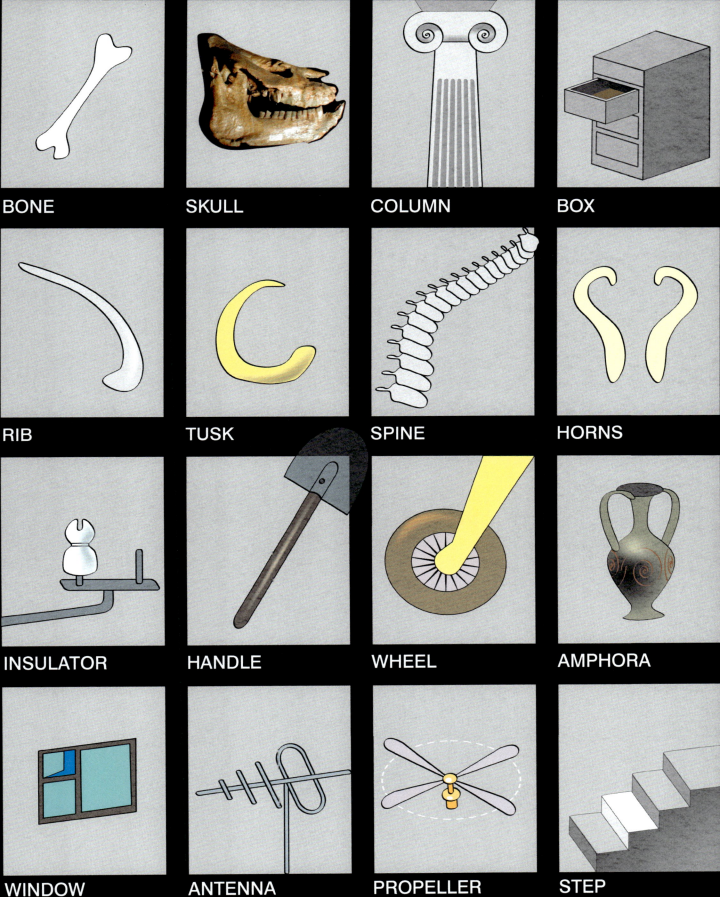

BODY

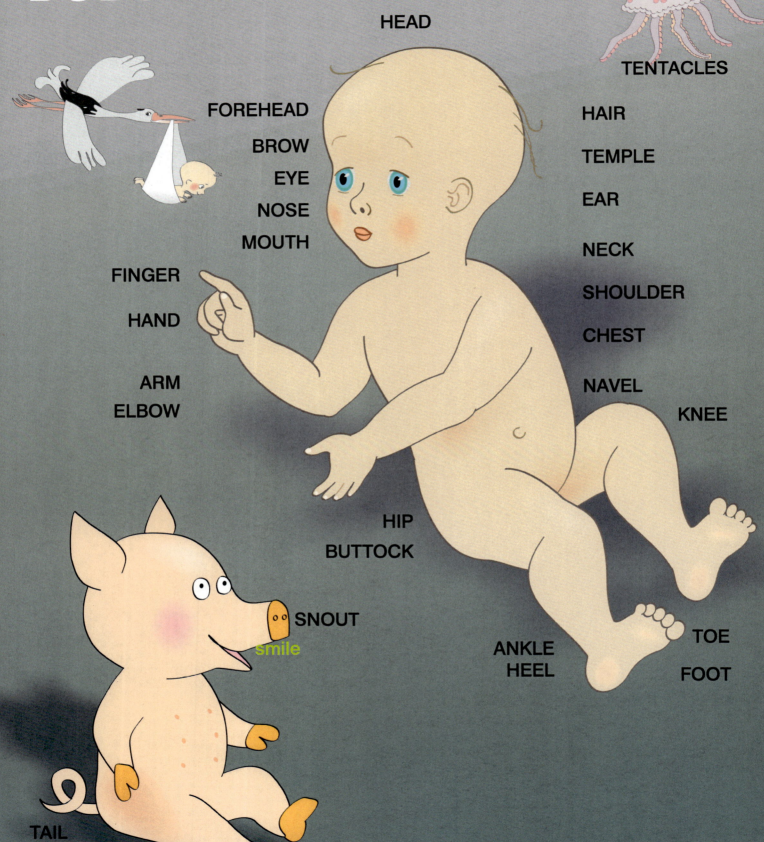

WING

WHISKERS

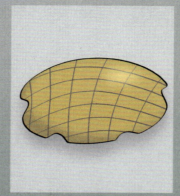
turtle SHELL

BEAK

TONGUE

TEETH

CLAWS

MUZZLE

SCALES

FEATHERS

snail SHELL

MANE

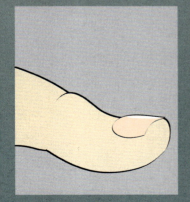
THUMB

TRUMP

HOOVES

PINCERS

39

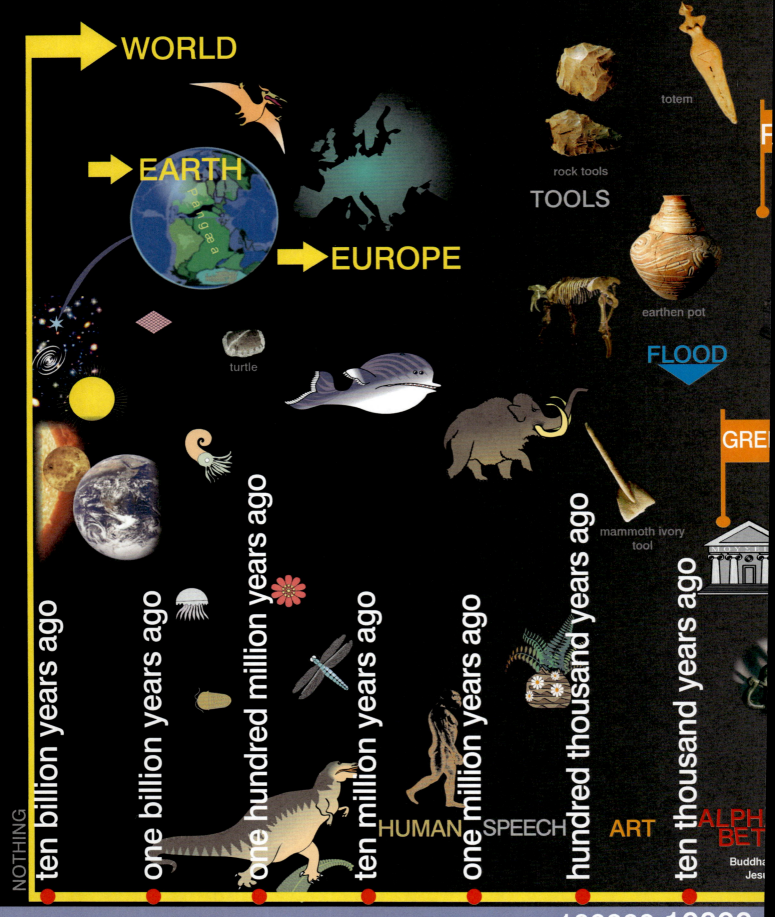

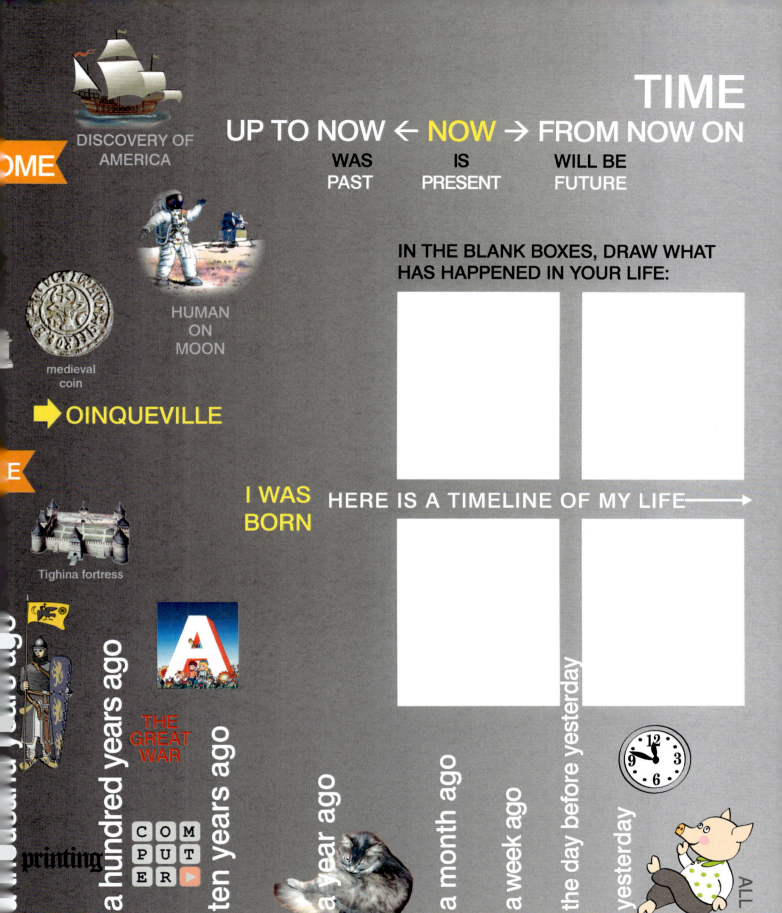

THE MAKE-UP OF EVERYTHING
OR WHY MYLKEE IS ALWAYS HUNGRY

A FOREST

WHAT A NICE AND EMPTY PLACE!

WHY EMPTY? THERE IS A FOREST!

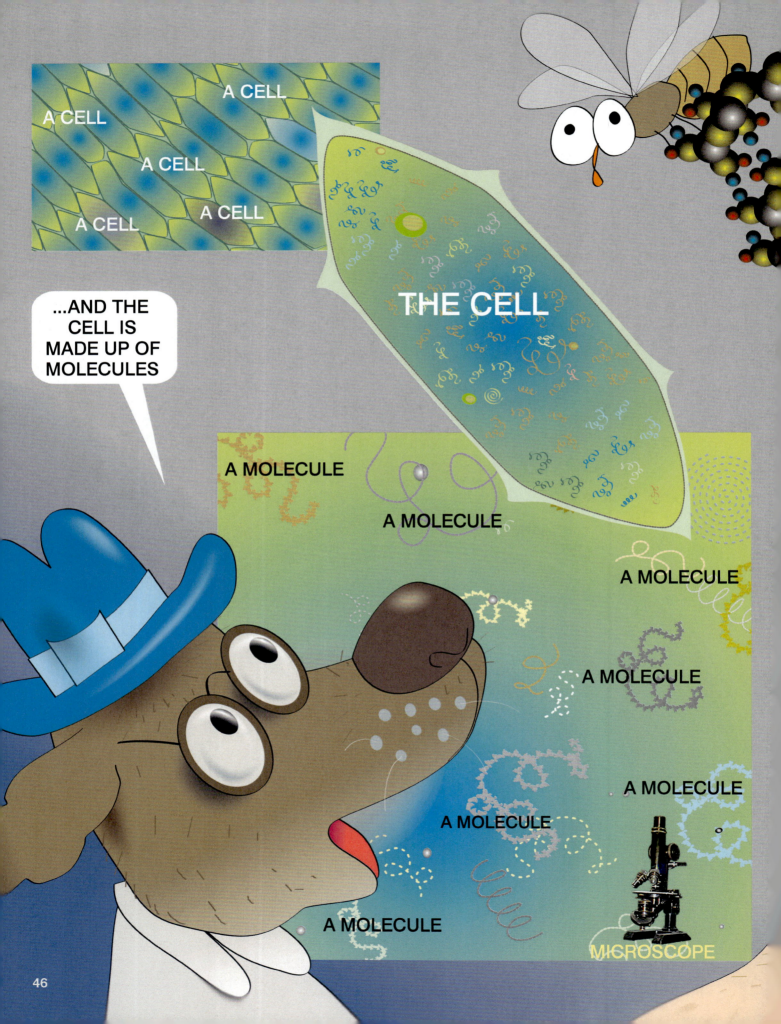

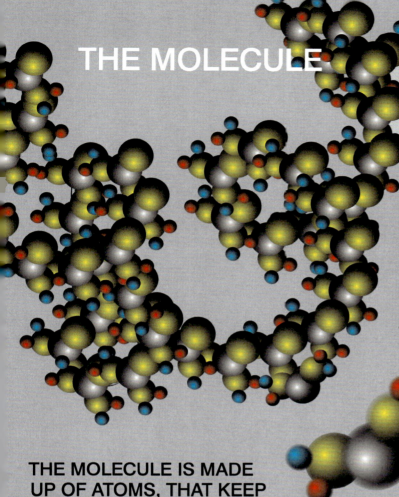

		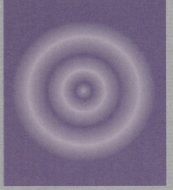	
ALL	SOCIETY	INDIVIDUAL	CELL

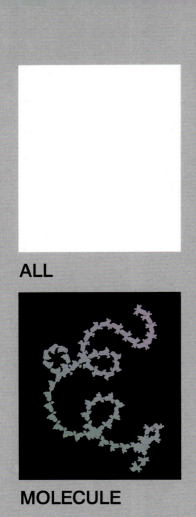

MOLECULE	ATOM	PARTICLE	NOTHING

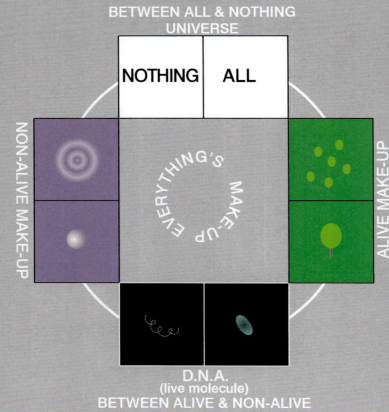

Scientists say there are four powers that keep things together: GRAVITY power keeps together the Sun, Earth, Moon, stars and so on; ELECTROMAGNETIC power keeps together molecules; STRONG nuclear power keeps together atoms; WEAK nuclear power keeps together particles.

CONFUSING

WONDERING   EXPLAINING

ONE PERSON

TWO PEOPLE

THREE QUESTIONS

FOUR LEGS

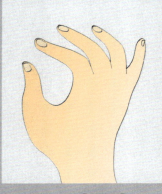
FIVE FINGERS

SIX TRIANGLES

SEVEN MOONS

EIGHT SWALLOWS

NINE STARS

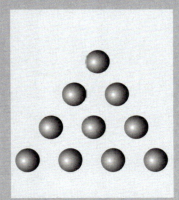
TEN ATOMS

ELEVEN FLIES

TWELVE HOURS

THIRTEEN STONES

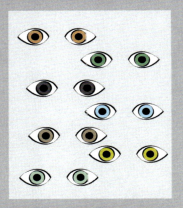
FOURTEEN EYES

FIFTEEN LEAVES

SIXTEEN COLORS

THE CASTLE OF KING STEP

Once upon a time Prof. W.W.Woof took our folks for a hike at King Step Castle.

They climbed the stairs higher and higher. Each one climbed on a top of a tower, and thought himself to be at the highest point.

Even Prof. W.W.Woof couldn't tell who was the upmost.

I'M AT THE TOP!

I'M AT THE TOP-MOST!

I'M THE HIGH-EST UP!

I'M ABOVE ALL!

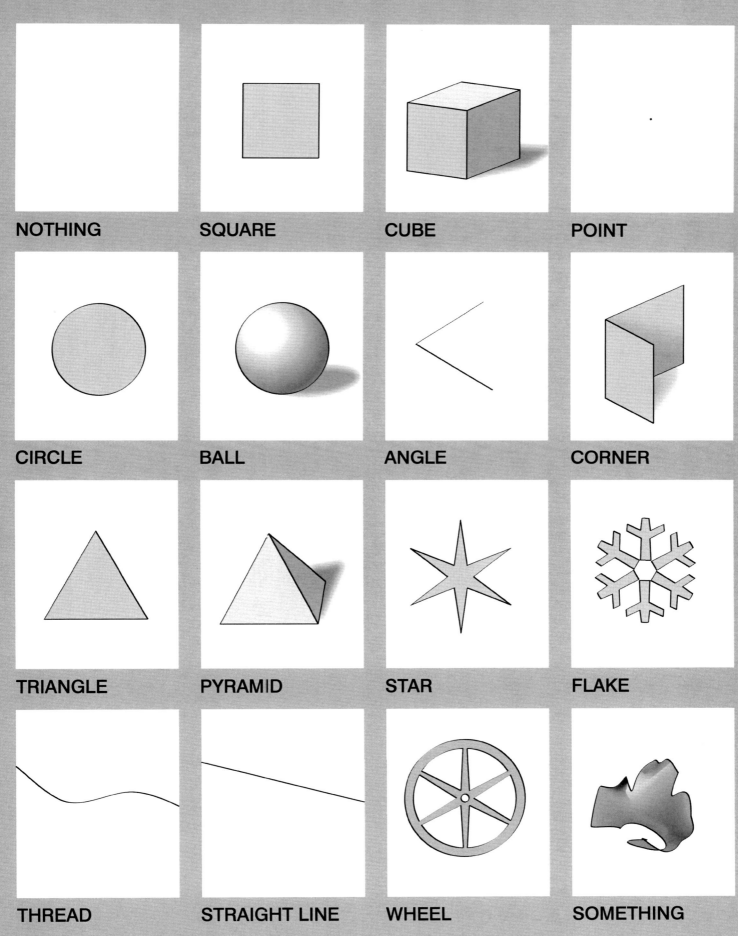

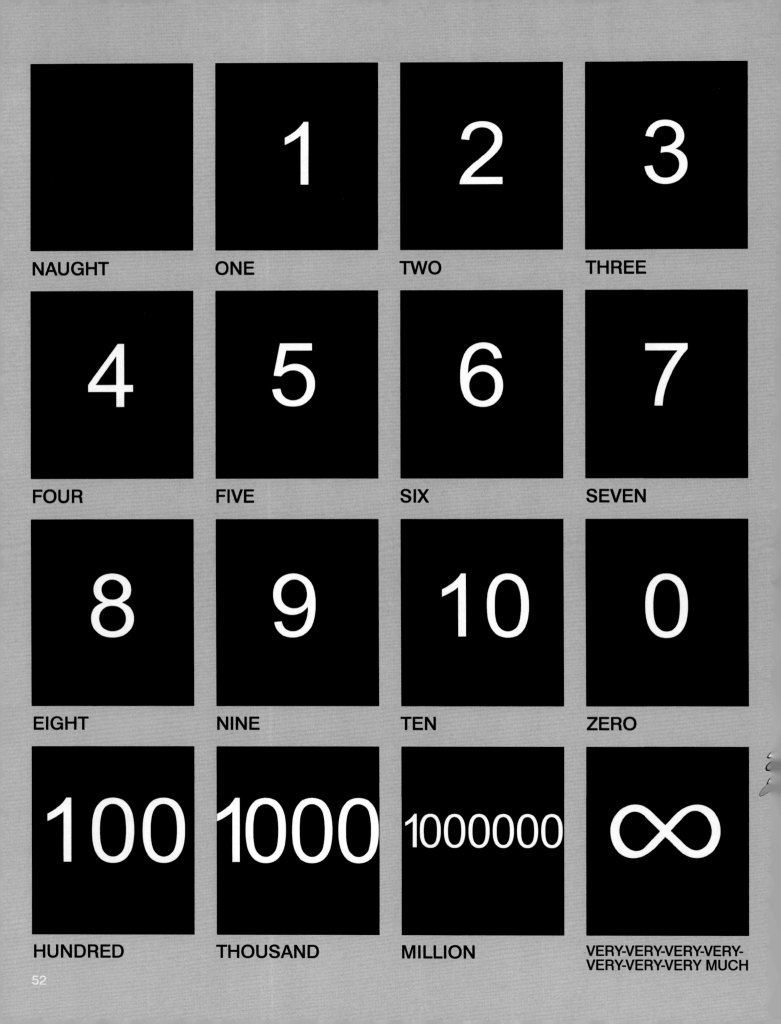

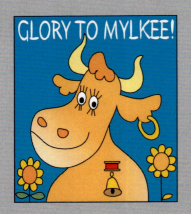 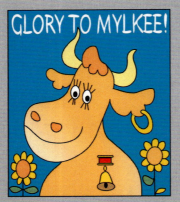 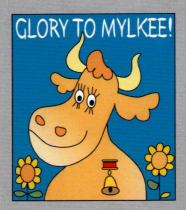 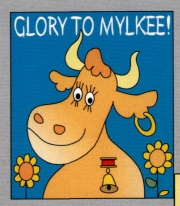
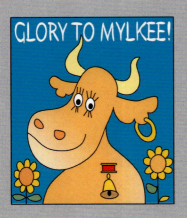 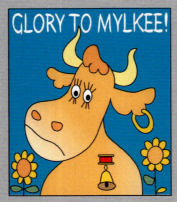 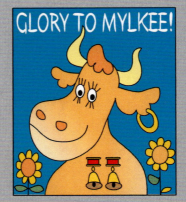 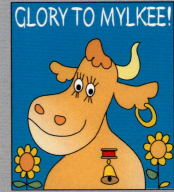
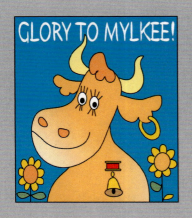 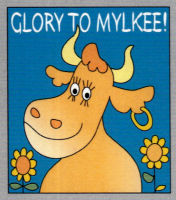 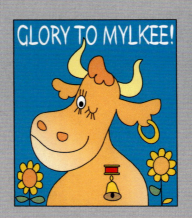 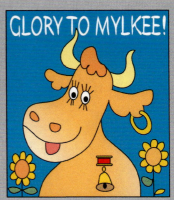
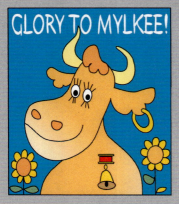 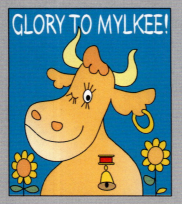 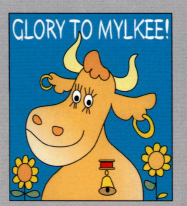 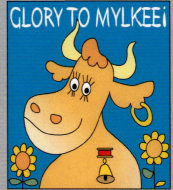

A poster was issued to mark the award of the Great-Brass-Bell-on-Neck to Mylkee.

THE EARTH

The Earth, Sun and Moon travel around the Galaxy in 20,000 years.

'GALAXY' means 'MILKY' in Greek.

The surface of the Earth is made of water and land — mostly water. There are four large stretches of water named 'Oceans': Atlantic, Indian, Pacific and Arctic. The large stretches of land are called 'Continents': Africa, Europe, Asia, North America, South America, Australia and Antarctica.

People divide the oceans into seas and continents into countries. Seas and countries can be very large and very small — depending on people's will. Sometimes they do not agree and fight among themselves to change the division.

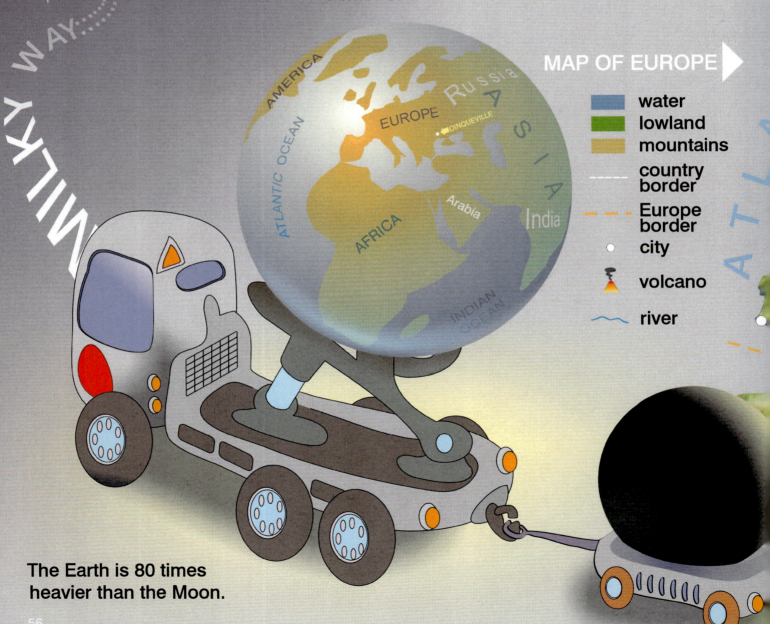

MAP OF EUROPE ▶

- water
- lowland
- mountains
- country border
- Europe border
- city
- volcano
- river

The Earth is 80 times heavier than the Moon.

 CAKE
 CANDLE
 BALLOON
 HUT

 DIAL
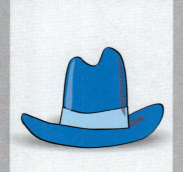 HAT
 STOOL
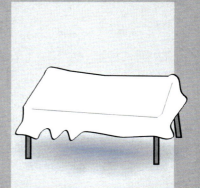 TABLE

 CHAIR
 CHIMNEY
 HOUSE
 LADDER

 BASKET
 GREETING
 HOE
 SPADE

 MERRY-GO-ROUND
 SHADE
 BELL
 KENNEL

 HELICOPTER
 SAW
 POT
 HOOK

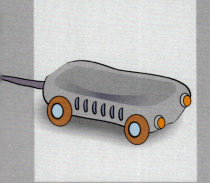 TRAILER
 AXE
 PLANE
 TRAFFIC-LIGHT

 CAR
 CURTAIN
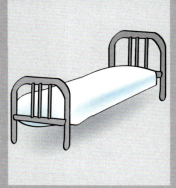 BED
 BABY CARRIAGE

PILLOW	SYPHON	UMBRELLA	POUND
BAG	OVEN	BRUSH	GRAIL
JAR	SICKLE	GLASS	SAUCEPAN
FLAG	BOW	SLEDGE	JUG

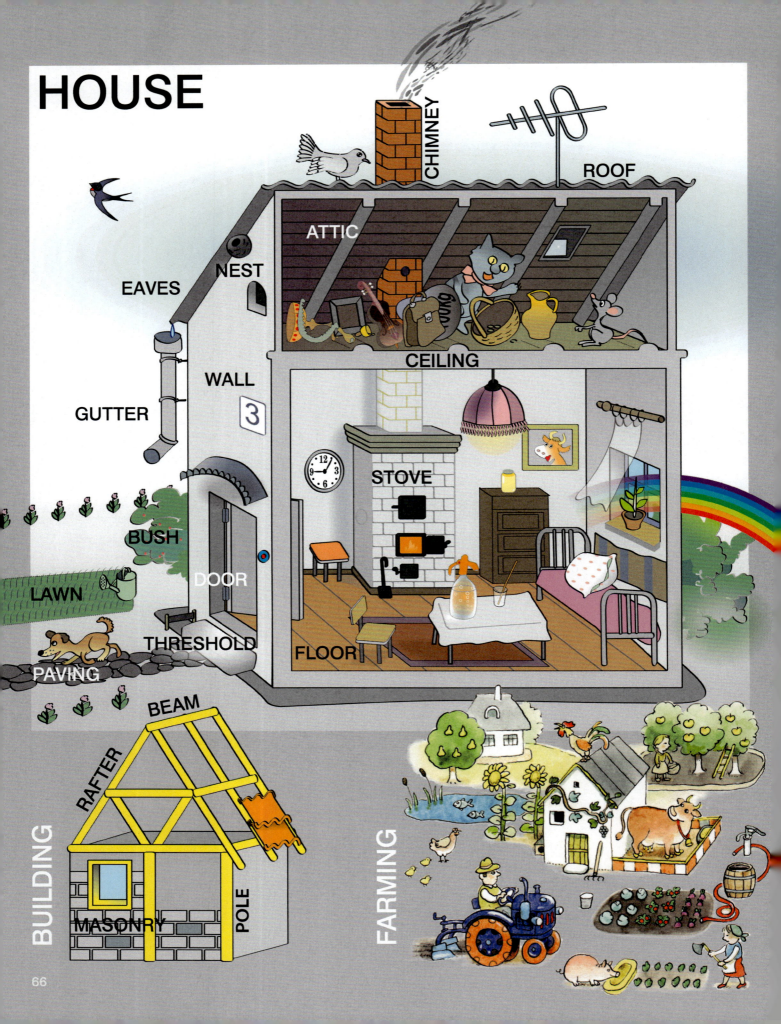

JOBS

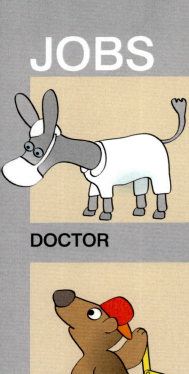   

DOCTOR   **PAINTER**   **SCIENTIST**   **ENGINEER**

CARPENTER   **TAILOR**   **COOK**   **MUSICIAN**

SMITH   **ASTRONAUT**   **BUILDER**   **FISHER**

WELDER   **WATCHMAKER**   **GARDENER**   **SWEEPER**

TOOLS

 DESIGN

 BOOK

 PORTRAIT

 STETHOSCOPE

 VIOLIN

 LADLE

 SCISSORS

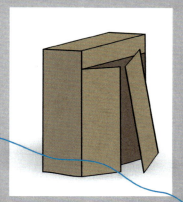 SHELF

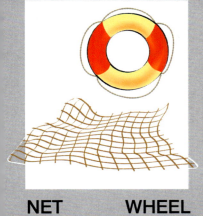 NET   WHEEL

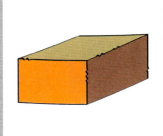 BRICK

 HELMET

 ANVIL

 BROOM

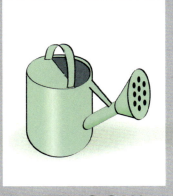 WATERING CAN

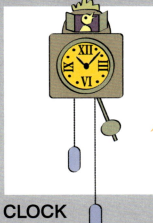 CLOCK

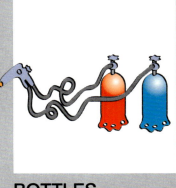 BOTTLES

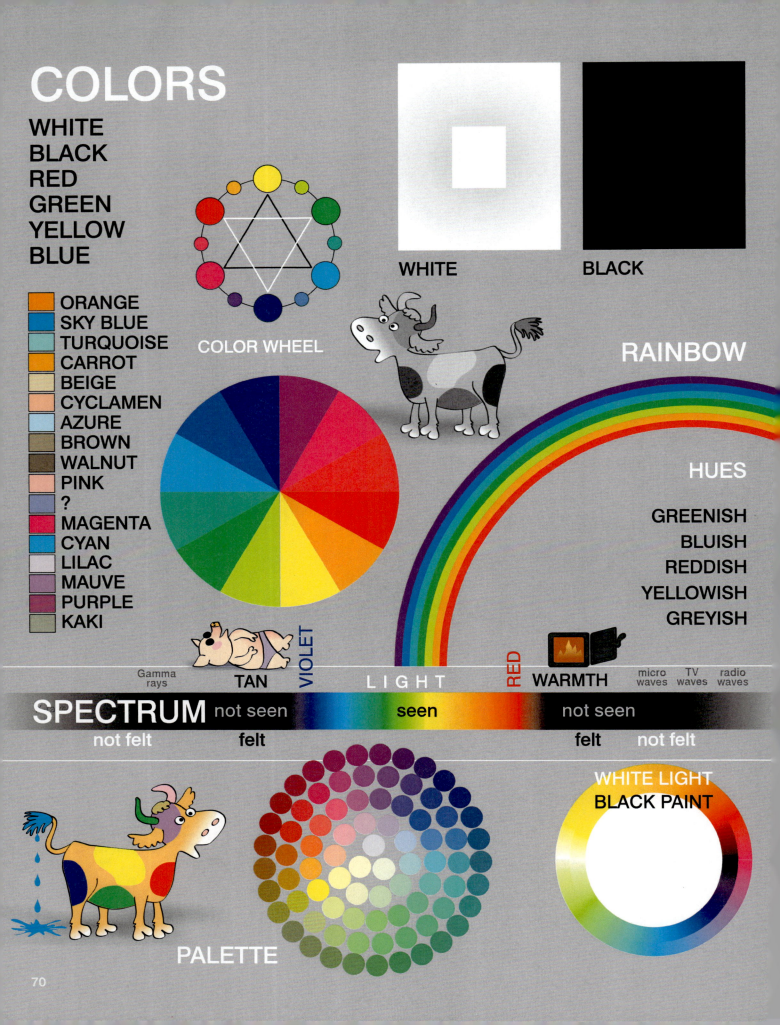

LETTERS AND ALPHABET

PROF. W.W. WOOF TAUGHT HIS NEPHEWS ALL THE LETTERS OF THE ALPHABET.

THEN HE TOLD EACH ONE TO CHOOSE THE LETTER THAT SUITS HIM BEST.

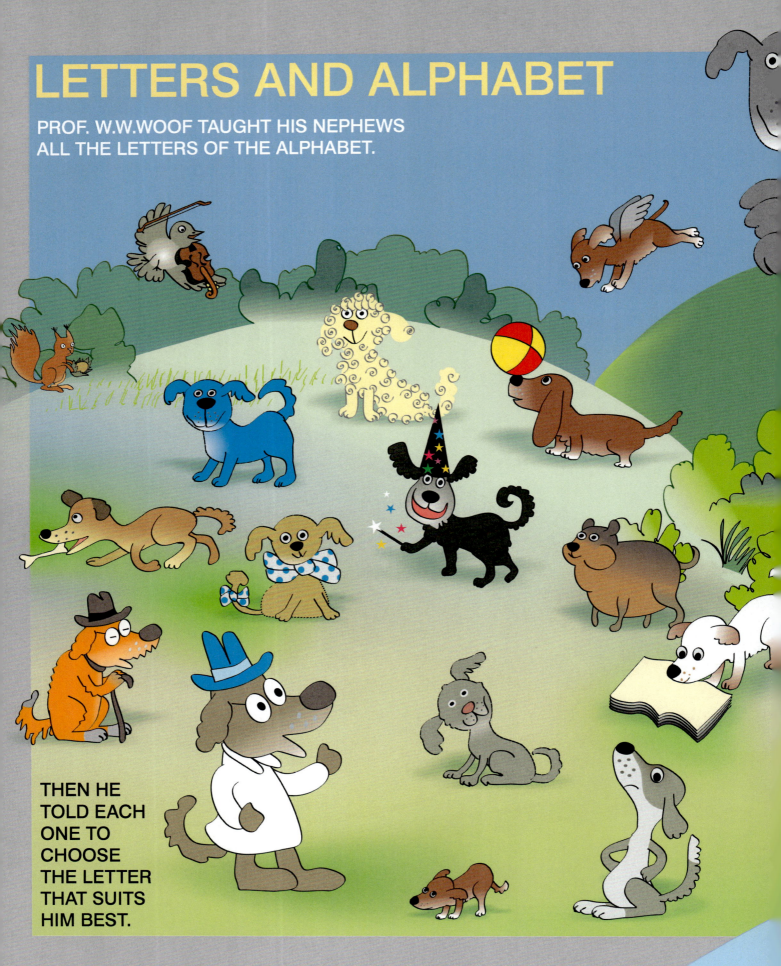

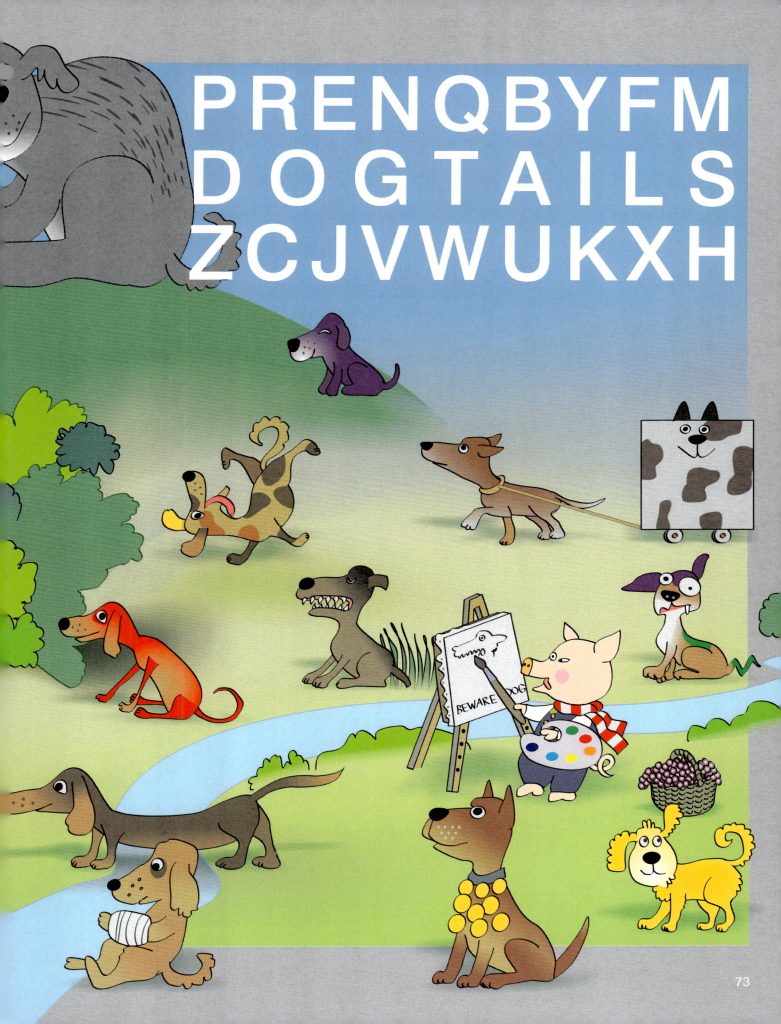

THE FIRST ONE TO CHOOSE WAS THE ANGRY PUP.
HE WAS MUCH ASTONISHED AND ASHAMED WITH HIMSELF.

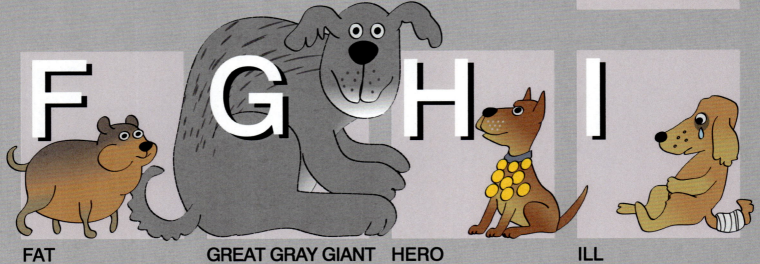

FAT GREAT GRAY GIANT HERO ILL

NAUGHTY OLD ORANGE PROUD QUICK

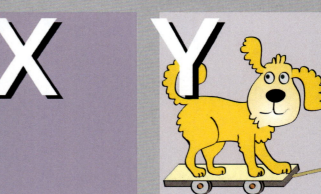

VIOLET WHITE WISE YELLOW

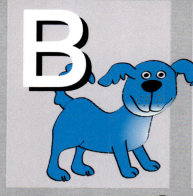
BLUE

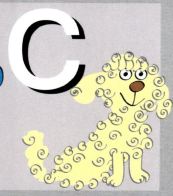
CURLY CUTE

DARLING DANDY

ENTHUSIASTIC

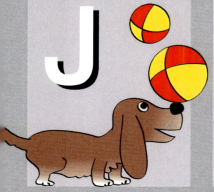
JUGGLING

KAKY KIDDISH

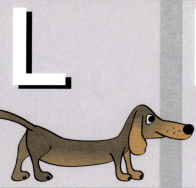
LONG

MERRY MAGIC

RED

SQAUARE SPOTTED

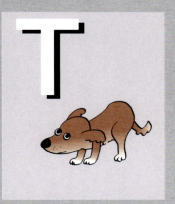
TEENY TINY TIMID

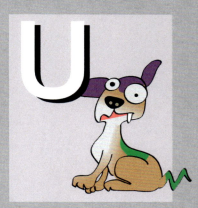
UGLY

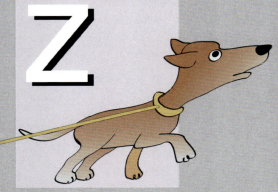
ZEALOUS

ONE LETTER WAS PICKED BY NOBODY.

WHY?

ONCE UPON A TIME...

RACE GAME

For this game we need a dice or a spinning top with numbers, and buttons of different colors or shapes—one for each player.

The players cast the dice (or spin the top) and move their buttons forward as many steps as the number shows… If, when moved, you land on a yellow circle—you miss your turn; if on a green circle—you take six more steps forward.

When you reach a circle with an arrow you should move your button where the arrow points. If you 'catch an Evil Mirror Splinter' (circle 57) you have to start from the beginning.

The game starts at Gerda 🔴

The one who gets to Kay first wins 🔵

In a large town, where there are so many houses and inhabitants that is not room enough for all the people to possess a little garden of their own, and therefore many are obliged to content themselves with keeping a few plants in pots, there dwelt two poor children...

TOP

DICE

matchstick

dice cut pattern

WONDER

THE SNOW QUEEN

by H.C.Andersen

Listen! We are beginning our story! When we arrive at the end of it we shall, it is to be hoped, know more than we do now. There was once a magician! a wicked magician!! a most wicked magician!!! Great was his delight at having constructed a mirror possessing this peculiarity, viz.: that everything good and beautiful, when reflected in it, shrank up almost to nothing, whilst those things that were ugly and useless were magnified, and made to appear ten times worse than before. The loveliest landscapes reflected in this mirror looked like boiled spinach; and the handsomest persons appeared odious, or as if standing upon their heads, their features being so distorted that their friends could never have recognised them. Moreover, if one of them had a freckle, he might be sure that it would seem to spread over the nose and mouth; and if a good or pious thought glanced across his mind, a wrinkle was seen in the mirror. All this the magician thought highly entertaining, and he chuckled with delight at his own clever invention. Those who frequented the school of magic where he taught spread abroad the fame of this wonderful mirror, and declared that by its means the world and its inhabitants might be seen now for the first time as they really were. They carried the mirror from place to place, till at last there was no country nor person that had not been misrepresented in it.

QUEEN   DRAGON

PRINCE-CHARMING   STALLION

 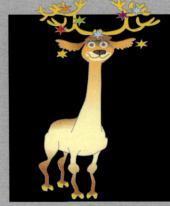

DWARF   MAGIC-STAG

QUEEN-OF-ANTS   PRINCESS

DUTCH CHEESE

 ELF

 GOBLIN

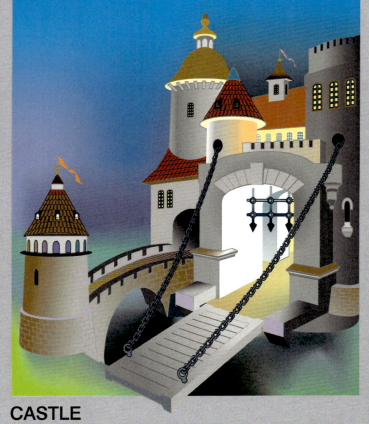

 HUNTER

 FAIRY

CASTLE

 WIZARD

 KING

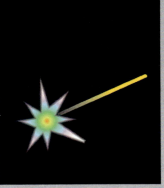 MAGIC-WAND

 WITCH

 GOLDEN-APPLE

 OGRE

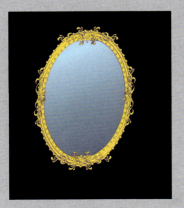 MAGIC-MIRROR

 CINDERELLA

WARCRAFT

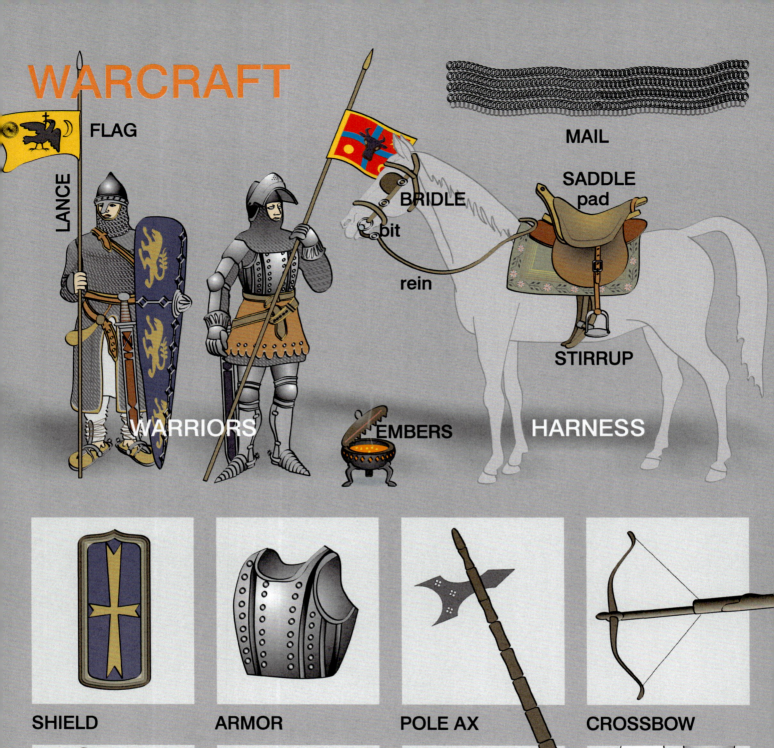

FLAG
LANCE
MAIL
SADDLE pad
BRIDLE
bit
rein
WARRIORS
EMBERS
STIRRUP
HARNESS

SHIELD

ARMOR

POLE AX

CROSSBOW

SWORD SHEATHE

CANNON

cannon BALL

SHOES

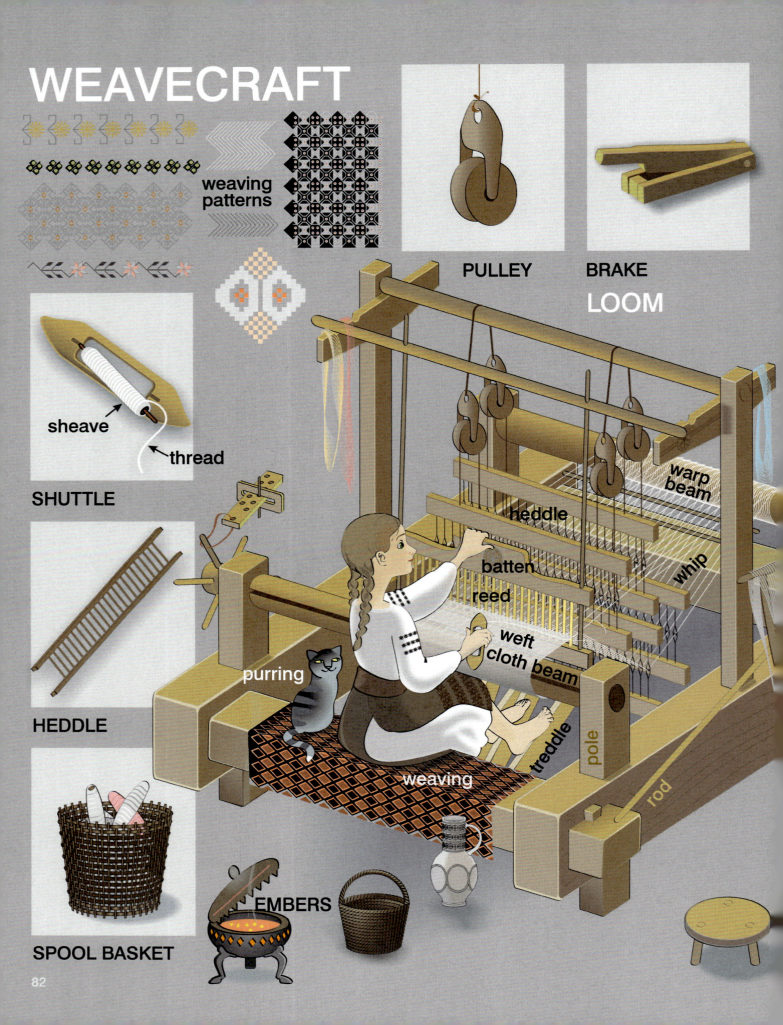

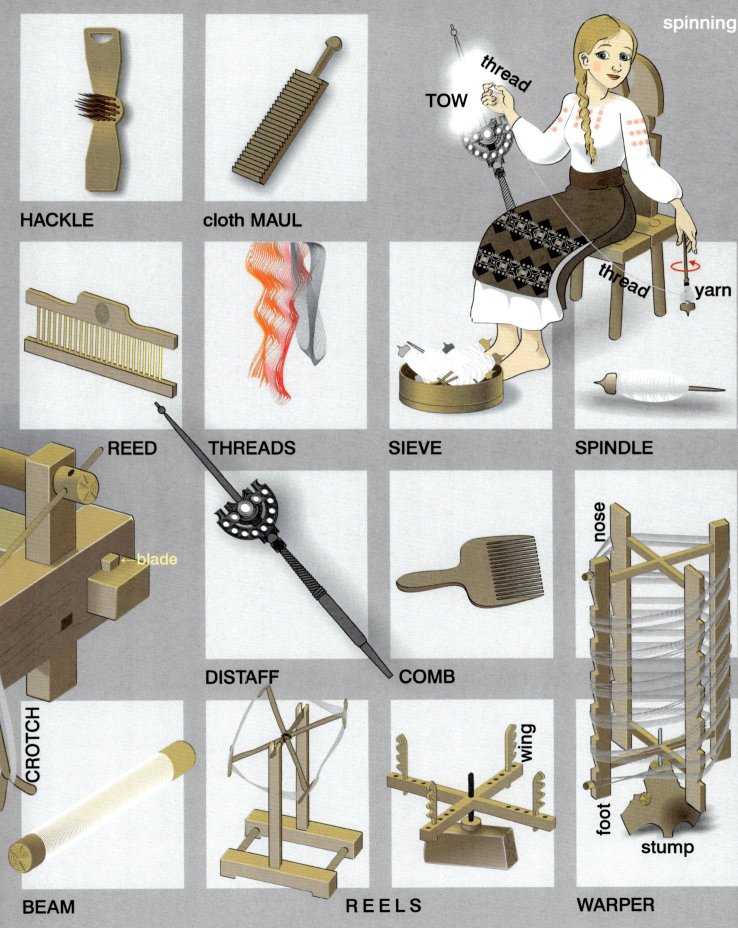

SO – OTHERWISE

GOOD – BAD
NOW – THEN
BEAUTIFUL – UGLY
IF — THEN
CLEAN – DIRTY
THEN – IF
SATISFIED – HUNGRY
WISE – SILLY
TRUE – FALSE
KIND – EVIL
CLEVER – FOOL
SMART – DUMB
PITIFUL – WRATHFUL
BOLD – COWARD
GENEROUS – GREEDY
CLEAR – CONFUSED

Everyone takes a button (the same one as in the Snow Queen Game) and quickly climbs up to the 3rd floor, where Mörl Klimber is waiting with a chewing gum award.

Cast the dice on your turn, and then climb as many steps as the dice shows.

You may stop on your way (if you wish) at the yellow steps to give the lady a hand, but you lose your turn. At the red step you would (of course if you are not against it) turn back and start from the beginning.

The game's name OINQUE-OINK is an unregistered trademark of P.Oinque.

WE ARE SO WILTED!

I'VE STRAYED! FORGOTTEN MY WAY OUT!

START

shadow

DO I MIND?

I feel
I think
I doubt
I hope
I know

I don't mind
I don't bother

FEEL
BELIEVE
AWARE
HELP
WISH
CARE

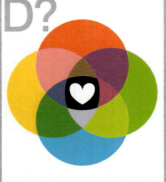
HEART

DEAD

ALIVE

BIRTH   LOVE

FEAR

RIGHT	TRUTH	GAIN	LINK
WRONG	LYE	LOSS	MESS
LOOK!	CHOOSE!	TAKE!	SEE!
ANGER	DOUBT	PRIDE	PASSION

MINDFULL   WONDER   LIKE   PITY

greed : want
hate : don't like
ignorance : don't care

SHADOW OF THE SHADOW

ONCE UPON A TIME

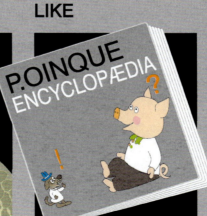
THERE IS

WOULD BE

CONTENTS
FOR GROWN-UPS

NATURE

The roundabout world Scaling relationship Space	4 — 7
Objects, notions Difference, generalization	8 — 9
Animals, birds, fish Environment	10 — 17
Growth, development Plants, botany Insects	18 — 19 28 — 31
Life Biology	32 — 33
Evolution Scientific research Paleontology	34 — 36
Divisible and undivisible Individual, body	37 — 39
Time Calendar, history Macrocosm and microcosm	40 — 41
Matter	42 — 48
Abstractions Mathematical objects Paradox Analysis and reason	49 — 55

HUMAN WORLD

Geography Social relations Emotions	56 — 62
Artifact Craft	63 — 69
Colors Properties Symbols	70 — 75
Communication Appreciation, imagination, fiction Mythology, history	76 — 83
Ethics	84 — 85
Consciousness	86 — 87

Made in the USA
San Bernardino, CA
21 December 2018